VISITING LIGHT

VISITING LIGHT

Jean Earle

POETRY WALES PRESS
1987

POETRY WALES PRESS
56 PARCAU AVENUE, BRIDGEND,
MID GLAMORGAN

British Library Cataloguing in Publication Data

Earle, Jean
Visiting light.
I. Title
821'.914   PR6055.A694

ISBN 0-907476-76-7

Author photograph: Stuart Smith
Cover painting: 'Painting About A Landscape' by
Ernest Zobole

Published with the financial support of the
Welsh Arts Council

Printed in 10½ point Garamond by
The Camelot Press, plc., Southampton

CONTENTS

THE WOOLLEN MILL

What we are hangs upon that moment —
Which *will* come —
When the cross is taken in the warp
And the weave is certain.

On the drying-ground
Where the wet wools are hung to blow,
Scarlet, blue,
I was first aware of a true pattern.

To do with light....

It was an overwhelming addition,
Seeing, prepared in light,
How the warp lay. I had to go and sit down
Behind the carder, trying to come to terms.
In the pile of fluff lay a dog
Asleep. Between his half-closed lids
Light sparkled — even there,
In the dreaming eye.

Down the mill wall, light translated water,
The roaring silver
Over the wheel, that groaned out light — and light —
Danced out of ancient cogs
From when they were young wood.
Such bright looking hurt —
When someone passed,
I turned my head for relief of his shadow.
But he left two fish
On the window-sill — and they burned light,
Drew it into their stillness
Like a great cry. Blinding silver.

The man dressing a loom was all afire
With fused intent, passing down arms and fingers
Into his skilful moves.
As in a thrown shuttle
I watched the visible mix
Between his light of mind and the silverlit water
Working outside. At that time
The mill was run by water —
In dry weather, the wheel stopped
But then, against such interval
A mountain of wool was dyed
Scarlet, blue —
So that, when rain came,
There would be plenty of warp
Ready to take the cross.

It was the season when the natterjack
Comes to water, carrying her mate
(Or so they did on my farback nameday)
And as they processed,
All the light in the sky flew
To touch flashpoints where the webbed feet
Displaced moisture; tilted instant mirrors,
Killing all dark spaces
Between flowers. Marsh buttercups —
And those fill up with light,
Even in thunder.

Look back, from evening. A widespread day
Maddened yet silked with light.
Toads assembling —
Wool blowing unbearable keen colours,
The two fish burning

Scissors of light. The weaver took them home
To his shut house. The mill shut down.

I suppose every turn of the earth
Is loom to someone's light.
A skein untangles
Out of wind and sun,
Lies in the ordered warp, patterning
Scarlet, blue —

The cross taken.

A stage in warping a loom is known as "taking the cross".

VISITING LIGHT

A single rose-red tile
On an opposite roof
Comes and goes among adjacent slates,
According to light, weather.
Rain, blown off the spring river,
Brings it up proud
Of surrounding greys —
Like an expected face, flushing.

Roofs fascinate —
How they straddle families,
Equal across the too-many
As over the so-lonely,
Give nothing away.
Discreet above violent stoves,
Cold or much-tumbled beds —
The small saucepan with one furtive egg,
All he can or all he will
Allow himself — which?

Here broods a latent poetry
Nobody reads.
The weed that has managed flowers,
Pinched in a crack,
Lays its thin shadow down
In the afternoons; as a new mother will,
In the room below.

Jackdaws are in these chimneys.
Their difficult lives
Reflect our own; but who will be awake
For the luminous dawn
When the young fly for the first time?

Jackdaws seem to be inimical
To the mosses, disrupt them down
To me, as I clean my step,
Rubbing with bluestone in the old way.
My scour against the world's indifference
To important symbols — the common roof,
Likeness of patterns.
How warm this moss is,
In my cross hand! A miniscule forest
Full of see-through deaths
That should have had wings....

"Under one roof"
Is such an old expression,
Steady and parental —
Yet life beneath,
Hidden by the roof, changes pace
Daring and malicious as jackdaws,
Unpredictable
As visiting light: or the one rose-red tile
Flushing up — vanishing.

NOTHING — AND SOMETHING

At the house corner
A cling of cat hairs
Stayed up on breaths of noon
Rising and falling —
Tongued out of her garment
As she rolls in flowers.

She, too, is the colour of marigolds.
Of this cat's mark upon the world
Nothing visible save one eye
And, up there, the catch of hairs
Gesturing. Wilder than a web —
Which would be common to the wall,
Part of it. This fanciful weave
Becomes the question
Bloating all things discarded.

It opens like a cage,
Streams out in tension —
Stretches a pure Picasso throat
Towards light; then falls,
Limp from the point of catch,
Succumbed.
For an instant, the breeze lent it menace,
Reproach. The lazy watcher made of it
Delicate outline of a face.

What is the fate of such a cast-off?
Which, for the dreamer, sketches on air
Attitudes: of a lost cause,
A poem out of time,
That face...?

If it outlasts winter
It may become involved
With a nest — highjack a seed.
On days like this, millions loose parachutes....
Or cripple flies
Of the finest small-engineering precisions
That yet, hardly ever, know the way out.

Or the hard rains may parge it thoroughly
To the wall roughcast
And for such likely fate
Again the throat shapes poignant —
An anguished net flung about
Places of the mind
Without sleep or hiding....

The cat emerges from the marigolds,
Her silk trousers
Tacked with ruined ephemera,
Displaced ants.

AFTER THE CONCERT

At the hotel, for supper.
The famous quartet there,
Eating like ordinary men —
But half-an-hour since radiation
Beamed along their bows, a magic eye
Probing a small-town audience.

We were two music lovers seldom indulged —
And had been close to tears.

The big rooms flowed, one to another,
Lights, groupings. We sat together,
Smiling a little, watching the quartet —
Who took their supper
Into the end room and pursued
Some argument. One raised his resting cello
Out of its case, eager to demonstrate
And one played a lovely chord —
That floated above wine and chatter,
Fainting into glass.

All this was food to us,
We would carry it home. They were quite oblivious
Of people looking, wistful after joy.

Until a third shook out his different hair
(Compared with ours, how passionate
A statement!). Came on like a prince
Fronting an uncouth mob: and closed
The double doors.

EVERY DAY

Every day, something is given —
Even on black day, blind day.
As though a force,
Itself immune,
Indicates sudden balsam,
Consolation. Pain may continue
But the spirit lifts....

If only this flower —
Year by year, on the bare, northlit place,
Raising a single constant
Of piercing blue

Which may mark the grave of an angel
Such as (a visionary tells us)
Die all over the earth,
Not divinely protected
Like the great angels.
These patrons stand for us
Unarmoured.

Every day, some dissolution of fears —
A bright hand
Sweeping icicles. Instantly lost
But seen: given.

Even today — so bleak and rainy
We pull curtains and watch an old film
About jungle nature; the want of colours
Blessed with perceptive mirth,
Noting a tiger
Enfold her child — with the moon look
Into her paws, of a human mother.

A WELL GONE DRY

The well's empty —
Scrattled by insects of words
Manoeuvring soil-grains.
Patiently damped with feelers,
They will not adhere.

Suddenly —
The mysterious source (never surely located)
Seeps this light moisture. *Hoard that!*

It's thickly scummed —
And now a beast has trodden it,
There is the spoor.

Oh! upright out of sleep —
Dryness of tongue making water shapes
Out of whatever
It tries to say....
In such a dream, the mind's a bromeliad
Offering up its cup
Of natural tears.

Owners of wells
Assume integrities. They should not fail
Over personal traumas
Of running dry — but wait,
Calmly, for the ghost cloud,
Big as a man's hand.

Careful — don't get upset
Or give at the knees as that beast did,
Stumbled on promise of drink.
Don't taste for purity —
Don't even look!

Wells like Rebecca's —
Deep underground, going down ancient steps
Cut by the ancestors
Who dipped with confidence their large
Decorative vessels.
This well (and indeed, most wells)
Was never like that....

Now it is more than dry,
There has been frost.

But as a winter kills
Heart and fingers —
When, out of nowhere, faint
Across iced airs,
A scent of bluebells....

So with dry wells.
The dehydrated form,
Stretching its leather,
Feels in some taut nerve —
More steeled than stressed —
The cloud, as yet unseen.

The far-off rain.

REPORT FROM AFRICA

I

Another land and culture —
Yet we sit eye-to-eye
With this poor man telling his dark beads.

His interpreter moves
Unconsciously closer
To her subject. They embrace
And weep

And we, who never heard that tongue
Until we watched their tears,
Become interpreters.

2

The young black couple
Stumble in capture
Preceded by a child
With a dog on very short string.

Bright, bright the colours
Red shirt. Blue hat.
The onlooking world
Will notice the dog
Dragged across homework, chat,
Smells of supper.

Look, how the waste behind
Stretches, forever and ever —
Orange dust
Smiled with a brilliant wind.

CAPTAIN MORRIS'S PAVAN

The house fell. A new one rises
On the same ground: but style has changed.
Now and again, one who recalls it passes....

Silver on the sideboard. Big fires
To welcome guests
Honking up the drive
Which keeps its trees. Only last spring
The house stood — just stood.
In the long drawing-room
A sycamore full of birds
Pushed through rafters. Later, hung its keys....
Dealers had made off with the entrance door.

They brought the Captain back to his house
On a field gate. In his pink he lay
Under the sporting trophies and masks
Of foxes. A bardic huntsman
Took it into his head to pace the lawn,
Sounding a *"Gone away...."*

Over the blank doorway, the Captain's crest
Flowered at all seasons
And was a target for boys
Till the house fell.

GRANDMA'S HOUSE

Grandma, I come to you out of the night
In the loud street, with trams.
My legs trot down the tunnel
Into your courtyard —
It is like being born,
Dark and dangerous.

I have my grown-up fast by the hand.

For once, that street threw a bloody knife
Into your yard and Grandpa keeps it now,
Behind the clock.

Grandma — some people's fires
Seem warmer than others,
Children warming their knees
Become different. I am different
Because of you....
So memory makes us. The wooden plait
Round the barometer is as you wore your hair.
In my house now, I tap it for fine weather
And you are with me: sofa and hotter fire.

Again I finger the bead stool, obsessed
With its cool crunch. Its pattern was my fetish,
Never forgotten. "Bessie made it —
Dead before you were thought of!"
Her velvet lived
And her careful beads. All black and white —
Yet she was most untidy, you said,
And loved scarlet?
A child ponders such things. The barometer's plait
Is round your face, Grandma, ever a rising day.

There was another house on the way in —
Shuttered. Always the same grasshopper sound.
"That's Mr. Stokes, playing his violin —
He's a widower."
The two skills went together?
I puzzled — but never asked.
Whenever I meet a violin,
Mr Stokes is remembered.

BOY IN A CATHEDRAL

The white stick veers him past
Hindrance — or help —
With a bat's tensile avoidance.

Under the east window
Is his goal — roped from trespass,
But what does he care....

Where great festival choirs
Open the vaulted skull
And solo angels,
Noting his expectancy,
Sing above best

As though his blindness,
Waiting down there,
Offered them a huge flower....

He comes unguided
And is known to servers
Of the place. Tactful as its moths
They flit from his path.

Without eyes at all — not even shells
To bed them with — he clamps hands
Where sight should be: or gropes —
Blank to rubies of light,
Swags of colour —
Along the edge of staging, for some substance
Of what he loves.
Not finding it, he rocks
As a child will....

What can be done?

Any approach seems to belittle
His four exquisite skills,
Drawing on startled pity
Bluest inventions of his tongue.

PERSON TO PERSON

When you stand before me and look at me — what do you know of
what is inside me?

        Kafka

I have not stood at the storm's eye of your grief.
You have not tanged the very wry
Of my honey, where it turns to salt.
If you were to tell me — eagerly,
Using some catalyst of all tongues —
"I am here. *Here* — "
I might not know that place.

And were I to put my life into your hand,
Rolled small for you to grip around,
Tied with my knot,
My name for you stamped on the gift —
You could not read: for it is not your life.

Longing for absolute exchange,
The quick of depth retreats....

Because of this, shall we not touch to be
Most choice and careful of each other?
Reverent before another's joy or pain
As though playing host
In a house trustfully loaned to us.

We may not experience those beds, mirrors,
As in our own sure home —
But we admire,
Ardently sparing fragile things....

Overwhelmed perhaps, by a strobe light —
To realise it is an eye

Our lender sees with, prompts us to accept
Blinding intransigence by veiling sight.

AFTER THE GORSE FIRE

Stirred ash turns up glosses
Of beetle underparts. Fire licked off
Scurrying backs,
Spat away rainbow trims
Never noticed before. How they iridesce....

Sunk into root shadows,
Perhaps some equivalent of yellow
Pleasured a beetle's dark
As gorse in bloom livens the sad
Human eye?

Such yellow as that was
Lifts a dark looker
Clear off the hill, a child's height
Nearer the sky.
Webs under all, nests, a hot scent —
Another world: ruthless and wild
Like our world. And tinder-dry.

So pure a yellow
Floated, as though free of the hill
Holding it. A tuned ear —
Transposing yellow from the key of sight —
Seemed to hear water
Far off. Not raining and no river?
All so dry....

Yet the dog vanished; no more seen
Until a squirm over the prickled ground
Brought him out again,
Dripping his tongue.

That was yesterday. Purest yellow joy
Diminished now, the hill shrunk inward,
Blackened: as happy rooms were once,
If the old lamp darkened,
Turned too high.

The ear heard truly. There's our spring uncovered —
Lost under gorse when its innocent use
Went to the dark. Calling through web, nest,
Holocaust. The dog knew it
For a survivor. It falls out of the hill
Whatever burns to ash or flourishes.

THE SOURCE

Today has been like a shoe
Fitted too tightly,
Pressing a penitential band
Over the toes. Not to be eased off,
Because today required just such a smart,
Disciplined shoe.

Once, I saw Auden creep
In his mapped detail, out of that kind of day,
Back to America.
Early on, he had taken a small bag
Out of his mind and, during the formalities,
Kept it close to his surreptitious leg.
A well-used bag, blazoned ADIDAS....
Couldn't have held much — some lifesaver
For these occasions: a sponge, a few poems?
Perhaps — his death?

My bag holds always the same panacea
Against the test of pinching shoes and days.
The certainty that — at any moment,
However fraught —
Severn rises in Plynlymon's wilderness,
A handful of water stealing away
Through the lonely brown....

If it is not evening yet,
Evening will come.

SHUTTING THE BOOK

Up and down the tired Valley
He roared the old bike —

When he had petrol.

Every girl's friend,
No girl's lover. Little legs
And the beak of an eagle.

A hunchback.

In those times —
Old folk just looking on. The young
Sticking up out of their foundations
Like blunted nails —
His dark jokes, his sunny smile,
Bits of the bike tied on with string —
We laughed beforehand,
To hear him coming!

In the hall, for dances —
Never dancing.

Singing up at funerals
As though death were nothing.
At the shotgun weddings, standing best man,
Grinning a future....

One of the girls, leaving
To find work, cadged everyone's picture
For the album: was given his quip
In token. "My photo, love?
No, no — you'd never be able
To shut the book!"

PICCALILLI

Overheard on a bus —
"Between him dying and the funeral,
I papered the house...".

What was in her bosom,
Raging? At a peak time,
Did she go herself to choose patterns
Or send out for some?

A friend rescues old photographs
Off junk stalls. Fades of dead people,
Priced by the frames.
"Pity for them!" she says,
Making space on her wall.
One faintly-laughing group
Centres a baby, that's no more now
Than a tentative smudge —
Protective clasp, though,
Dark as ever, across its white frock.
All buttons sharp. The dog's eyes
Anxiously surviving.

My neighbour runs a vase
For invalid flowers,
The ragged and terminal.
Quiet, a little water, subdued light —
As we'd wish for ourselves.
Through her garden in heatwave
She moves like an ambulance.

Such quirks are collectable —
One goes about
Delving their origin: like trying pickles

To guess the recipe. Certain of salt,
Vinegar. Elusive in the brine,
Often unnameable,
The burning spices....

LONELINESS

Lawn-cuttings tossed —
As in disparagement — over a stunted shrub,
Not the kind they had thought
It would turn out to be. Insignificant,
Stopped flowers: one or two, at most.

The child standing beside this bush
Of her own sort. Holding fast
To their couple of sweets
They stood together
While, far below, a melancholy bugle
Tried and failed: yet it achieved
Perfect loneliness.

"Father — what's that?"
Distant answer. "The Boys' Brigade."

Whaleback mountain
Layering bracken, rowan,
To the edge of town. Down a dry slope,
Children whizzing on old cardboards
At the speed of light. "Hi — hurrah!"
How the one child
Wished to be one of them....

Sudden picnics,
Lugging a cooking-pot, onions,
Rags of the joint,
Over that mountain to a brook.
Diffident father leading the child,
Not really with her....
The mother would tie her head
Like a gipsy. They would make a fire.
Soup full of flies

Or wasps — but they rose above that,
Shedding, on puff-clouds of zest,
Trivial hang-ups.

Child and father were closer then —
One with the mother's
Scarf-of-the-day, they knew where she was.

Couch in a corner
Of the parents' room. (The child
Had unmanageable dreams.)
Wind off the mountain, breathing
Salt, fern, all night wafting
Through a balcony door.
Against its radiant pane,
Soon after dawn, a still moth-shape,
Terrible to the child. And sometimes —
Sometimes, the mother gliding
Lightly from bed,
In her white wings standing....

Stillness differs...
From flower to moth, from moth to mother?

She spreading her wings out — out —
To the wild airs. "Ah-h-h...".

Whatever she sighed for, entered the child,
Entered the father.
Separately feigning sleep,
They knew where she was....

OLD SILKS

The king asked us in: built us the narrow houses
With big windows. Our looms caught light
And ribboned silks. Sunrise, sunset
Flew from the shuttle's repetitive clack,
Inherent rhythms
Powered the downward beat on the weft.

Our cult of auriculas
Striped the thin walkways. Our yellow birds
Sang to an inch-marked candle —
Which was sweetest?
We were a company for catches and banners,
Bringing a bold life to Spitalfields.

Our children coughed — their silken lungs
Warped in the dry breath
Of silk-rooms. Wastings of thread —
Infected gossamers —
Gathered between floor boards,
Padding them with death.

Our lads had bright cheeks
From the continual fever
Of their calling. They marched out songs.
Engine-looms, Indian calicoes,
Rumours of Charlie — any cry would do.
The king was put out: sometimes a few
Got themselves hung.

And fashion changed — even remnants for kerchiefs
Out of favour. We became bagmen,
Crossing sweepers, thieves.
Our children's hands,
Coarsened with picking at brooms, oakum,

Lost their inherited skills.
Still they died young....
A trend passed on out of the drifted silks,
The skeleton looms.

ST LUKE'S DAY

A day begun with love
Before nightfall
Had touched death. St Luke's little summer.
We made wine from apples.
Heard of a birth,
Entertained friends. A sweet day....

Sunset hurled up the sky
Portents of wild gold. It was then —
The premonition. Our friends stood
Transfigured. Splendid coronas
Haloed their careless,
Kind goodbyes: each lifted hand and arm
Charged with extreme farewell.
An archangel's....

After they left,
We made a fire to warm us.
Watched it freak up
Beyond the glass eerily projected,
We out there beside it,
Among leaves and stones.
Waiting —
For what had not happened yet
But it would
And it did.
This memory....

It was the evening of St Luke's Day.

FULL MOON

Winter nights of our youth —
Moonlit nights
Before the moon was a place
Men had walked on.

Stopping to look at each other....

The culverts roared
Under the road
Water off sodden hills
Where summer,
Ferny and warm,
Had told us, once for all,
How we were made.

Moon-plated tips became
Pyramids — the wastelands Egypt,
A silver desert.

Coat buttons
Fingered by the moon. Cold hands
In one pocket....

Saying goodnight.
The neighbours' windows,
Moonlight-quick.
My face. Your face.

The shadow of your hat.

WIFE AND DOLPHIN

Sunrise gulls, each one glittered
On a raft of diamonds. The loosed rope
Shimmering....
And out between Cradle and Cat
To bait the pots. Brooding there,
Alone in the boat.

A hot-tempered man....

Sometimes he saw his wife's face
On the water-glare. He had struck her a blow
And she had left. Would never return —
That was her nature.

Lip-tide —
With a light haze, lifting —
Was her eyes' very colour. The gathered sea
Loomed, whitened, parted on Cradle and Cat,
Foundering over....

He would chat up the dolphin
That was pleasant with him.
Had it play stick
Like a dog; watched it take fish,
Flash, swallow — jokingly neat. He dived once
Under the silver flump of it,
Touched his hand to belly and flick,
Smiling snout.

It became his own
(But free — he wanted that)
Looking for him to sight and amuse it.
He too was entertained —
In morose depths, delighted.

Saving for a new boat,
He would take summer people out
To see his dolphin. Two went with him.
Showman types —
He soon guessed they had plans for it!

What to do? Temper made trouble.
Once he was sure of their intent,
He would go alone
Where the full greenswing
Sets away from Cradle and Cat,
Far out....

And play stick with the dolphin —
Hit it on the nose,
Hard. It would never come back.

That is its nature.

TAKING STOCK

When we first lived here, the little owl
Spoke from our apple trees, at dusk.
Sometimes, wild geese,
Changing marshes or ponds,
Wedged along darkness, crying
Links with the soul
We do not mention, more than we would
Sweating or private shames. We listened then,
Knowing man's wild affinity
With such a sound.
Years, since that signal woke us....

The soul, also,
Tangles in high wires.

Or we might walk to the bridge,
Sure of a heron fishing —
Matching our careful stance
To his stiff tilt. It was a game
Of loving skill, so that he did not scare.
His fish are gone.

There is a place overhill, where they say
A cuckoo is. He doesn't come this way
Any spring now.

Giants (of a gaunt beauty)
Stab with remorseless legs
Tender old fields. The rhythmic cables hang
Heavy and essential. Women and girls
On farms go out now, in the evenings.
Children play
Who used to plod, till bedtime,
Oldfashioned chores.

Profit: and loss. Still, now and then, the soul —
Experienced like an illness —
Fevers a need to stare
And stare and stare
Into uncluttered sky.

TIGG'S EYE

Falling loose downhill
Towards some place —
No place yet.
Will in time become a place —
But what?

Sunward-facing land about a farm
Long gone: and then
Cheap terraces, clambering around
Black works, choked in their throats.
All that demolished,
Waiting.

Hidden sun —
A few lads picking trash over,
A few men lurching,
In low gear, the rubbled paths
That lead nowhere.
And this triangle,
Green of a sort —
Old landmark here,
Some ancient goat patch
Or cabbage garden,
Spared from man's crush, deadweights,
Opened up now
By steel bulls charging
At derelict streets, timestrips
Shouting so narrow and so loud,
Silenced
Under obliterating scoops —

And this scarred too
But with moods of children.
Tins, a burst ball,

Still-standing ghostly stumps
Using scrap-iron.
An evanescent warmth
Airs up from weeds, momently suggests
A scent of health; breathes almost like a field
Against the sun's remoteness,
Its folk name.

QUAKERS YARD JUNCTION, 1950

Dirty, slow up-train
Tumbles off blackboys, white-eyed, red-lipped,
Logs under arm.

Pigeons clocked out of baskets.
Everyone gathers —
Even the man with nystagmus,
His second home the ticket office shadows,
Juts up his face....

And they are gone, silvery. An old engine
Butts at the water-stocking.
Bogie-bolster rusts and rusts away,
The siding dandelions
Blaze for place.

Now, that immaculate spark
Engineers ride about in — coasting like silk.
We glimpse their dinner, flashed on a cloth.
And then the four-fifteen — a fuss-pot!
Colliers bundling whippets
To Pontypridd races.
Schoolchildren, banging doors.

Waste off the footplates breathes
To meet pinks in the station borders.
Clove scent and oiled rags....
Trucks noisily travelling. Lewis-Merthyr,
Powell Duffryn, Ebbw Vale, Cory's....

About this time, the line dog
(Lives at the ganger's hut, was in a film
So does not speak to us)
Officially rounds sheep off the track,
Back to the mountain.

Over the bridge, to fetch milk
From the village. Waiting the signals' click
Against sunset.
Emerald and red
Sequins the echoing bottles...
Stars the long mind.

THE BURNING YEW

(Llanfihangel-uwch-Gwili)

A church
At the heart of the farms
Which are all around on the hills,
Sunlit.
The heart in shadow

As we expect of it.

Names on the stones
Are family ones,
Called out from house to field
Up in the sunlight.
Living names; called back to the heart
In a seasonal swing.

Is death the name for it?

And this old tree —
A dark angel —
Lifted on tangles of family names
To its great spread: someone has left
A trash fire
Too close. The yew is burning.

Its heart consumes.
When a wild rosebush
Dances, a hole full of sparks
Glows to the same puff.
Names flake up out of it —

Answering calls,
Released in homing veils

To the farms, sunlit.

46

A LATE SWIFT

Understanding the swift —
From the blotched egg,
The mother fallen briefly to nest
Like a dancer fainted...

To the tormented chick.
Hazards of drought, hunger,
Fratricide. Baked under heat
Of belfry tiles,
Jostled by the bells,

Holding out
And holding on
Awaiting feathers.

Not a moment sure

Till the natural shock —
Grip. Slide. Grip —
Feeling the clay of the hiding place
Crumbling....

Suffered alone.
Alone it must be done —
Down a dark chuteway
Into shining. Out. A-swoop up —
Free.

Understanding also
A voice out of my cloud.
Lucid, stressing the parallels.
"I SHOW YOU THIS...".

PETER DREAMING

Peter considers much, how it will be
Not to be: when no one is left
Alive on earth. He and his mates,
Brash in their time, byepass the shabby deal.
Accept...?

Nightly, inside the owl skull
Strung from a poster of Burning Spear,
Some creature starts its countdown — sinister
To a boy's tidal mind
At the flood of reality. Peter has accepted
More than his age can bear
Without tender naps. He dreams
Bursting asunder of the world. Sleepwalks
The small hours, clicking at retakes
Of the nuclear film.
Cramping on stills
White as flashed bird-lime —
Risers and strugglers
Fractured from each other
Into stunned solo. Thousands together.

Yet they are all one person —
Peter.

In the hedge once, a wasp nest
Potent with grubs. "Keep well away, Peter,
There may be fumes."

But the examined frame was beautiful —
Roughly heartshaped; not in flat emblem
But as the full heart in a body,
Ample....
Layered in hexagons, each one a home
Perfect for wasps. Angry but not evil —

The whole geared to the future of the grubs.

Where's the dynamic force of world-parents,
Dedicated hordes
Organised fiercely as wasps
To save Peter?

He dreams his father, clumsy with poison,
The deep, arrested groan
From the hexagoned heart....

Silence.

A REMOVAL

After long rains,
Beating open my window
I look away to the hill —
A house set in its fold.

Sometimes a hawk
Planes over that roof,
Down into grass.

She has gone — the solitary
Whom I seldom met,
Who seemed never to use
Her field or her front door,
Her windows always shut

Yet whenever I yearned to the hill,
I felt myself to be
Catching her eye.

All hindrance is removed!
I spread the flag of sun
Observed on her field,
As though I grew in her grass.
I *am* the hawk and sky.

Had I something against her? No.
And she knew little of me,
It was her probable stare
In my direction, that I evaded.
A stone outlook, lumpishly aimed —
Limiting me, who cannot tolerate
Prisons or tourniquets,
Neither would she (parlour-bred)
Fathom my tenure of her greens.

If we caught the same bus,
Heavy-laden, we would help each other on
Like any neighbours —
Now, I fly to the hill
Clear: nor need I feel,
More than the hawk or the wind,
Her absence there....

THE COMPANION

I, too, had a companion once,
Such as you describe — an unseen certainty,
Tactful in his stay.

At a time of bewilderment, winter.
Big child moving her small child
Endlessly between house and school,
Up to the shop and back....

Breathing for head room, heart room —
Clinging beyond reason
To the small child's hand: yet mute.

What was there to say?

The sky enormous, hard with fast clouds,
Daws falling in purple wheels
Upon the oaks. Storm hanging
But it would not break
Down from the thundrous head
Into the heart.

Then I was first aware
Of someone with me —
Always a step behind,
Keeping me company. As soon as I was sure

The rain fell,
Strong convulsions of silver.
The child played outside it,
In a blackberry dry
And the companion shielded her
While I raged.

I slept, afterwards,
Still as a chair, by the evening fire.

Time has done much: a late spring
Loosening all that ground. Coltsfoot rising,
Sun beside penny sun, as on wires to light....

Small child grown. Big child's foolishness
Seen to be growth also. Company plucked
Out of the very air
Of anguish. Who was it that came —
Under the storm-cloud fetched
And from the cleared sky gone?

PICTURES FROM A POOR COUNTRY

Symbols of Place

Figure: in a clay house
Magnificent with orange light.

Cave of the dead. Remote.
One skull with another
One bone on another.
Time after time, the sun
Rises on them, fiercely.
Time after time, the sun goes down,
Sealing their privacy.

The baobab tree
Roots the known earth.
A weed, at the foot of its immensity,
Speaks for mankind.

Native Crafts

Mats.   For one, for two,
        For the village rowdy.
Pots.   Large enough — not too heavy
        For a child lifting.

Mock-up of a man

Four reeds.
Upstanding
Sky-pointing
Womb-thrusting
Weapon ready

Heat of the Day

This is a beautiful room —
Floor. Shade. Water.
No words.

Priorities

All-purpose knife
Food

Roof
Children

Love...?

If I die before you,
Sing me....

STILL LIFE, FLOWERS AND GREENS

These thoughts
Are the deep jug of water
Where the flowers rest: far enough away
From the roots' cry.

Circulations, systems
Curving, feeling with one another
Not as we humans curve and grieve
But in their closed dimension
And wild stillness

Synthesised only
By the small gaze
Of the few, groping to scale away
Evolved eyelids; to glimpse, clearly,
Something other than thought-babble....

As between varied grasses
Glancing their plumes,
Between shadow and stem
On a windless day —
The faint pulsation.

These thoughts
Are the tentative link
We sometimes move to express
But our mind cannot. Never.
Loud as we are in loss,
Hot and unkempt in our mortal wounds,
Numb to translate
How roots communicate
Mutilation.

Still. Silent under sun and moon —
Green and the flowers of green,
They have not long
To be their own. Taken in and eaten.
Turned into flesh, into dung,
Changed: for our use
And the upkeep of animals.

So harvest goes,
No help for it. Why should we fret
For what we must consume — will snap loose
To decorate our tense shapes?

Churches
And geometrical rooms
Brides
The dead....

GRACE DARLING

Madam:
        I write in answer to yours
That you were kind to send. Yes —
The life is lonely. But since the Rescue,
Summer sailors come out to look at me —
In shoals, if there's a calm sea.

I was made able to do it and I did —
That's all. I was helping Father.
Now there are all these letters,
Even offers to marry me!

Since you ask,
I am of low height and narrow build.
The pink dress they will show
After my death, is a loose fit
Though it might seem skimpy.

Our view? Inland towards Bamburgh,
Outward across the Farnes and the North Sea.
Everyone knows but they like me to say so
In writing. I hope to write neatly.

There's more work, with all this interest.
I find it strange —
I could have sat in a boat
On the London stage! Without asking,
They've made a song about me.

Hard to find time for fame.
The Longstone, you know, is like a ship —
Scrubbing and rubbing
Glass and brass every day and picking up birds
That kill themselves at the Light —

Which I shall do: being never robust,
Except on that night.

I'm twenty-two.
Four more years and I'll be
Under the tomb, my likeness on top for you —
Since I keep none by me
That I could send. Stone hair flowing,
That I always coil so tight
Against visitors. The carved seaweeds
Down my pillow trailing.

More as it was before the famous Rescue —
Nobody raving but the sea.

LOOKING IN

A documentary
About a desert. We sit relaxed,
Unshaded eyes learning that torrid floor.
Marvellously graded stones —
Head size to ball size
Through pearl-small, fining to dust.
The desert wind
Over and round them sings —
We are in the heart
Of the sandstorm, without being blinded.

Then to switch off — go out.
Tonight, a mackerel sky,
Graded crescendos of fleece, away
To diminuendo. Serried beneath the moon,
Motionless shells. Pearls....

Could we position the cloud
Over the stones,
Might the completed jigsaw
Point us a sudden strike
Into eternity? As when
Leaves and birds and a companion's hair
Blow all one way; a chord
Brightly sustained — then slipped,
Like a forgotten name.

Sit in again, for the News.
March with this evening's people,
Out in world-thousands, patterning
Grief and excitement, fear —
Graded from huge 'O'
Through the extremes of hate
To dying aperture.

Note what intricate lace
The seismic needle vandykes,
Screening an earthquake's passion.

High up, an aircraft
Scanning the devastation,
Photographs jigsaw truths
Of a city's death,
Repeats the needlepoint's
Fairylike art to stun —
Its dainty chaos.

SORTING JUMBLE

Respite here. Escape here.
As newt in pond
Feels the uprising springs
Bubble, prick, against its suspended form.
"Where are you, why don't you jump? ZZzzzz...".
But the newt's camouflaged. A stone.

Stand-easy here. Chair folding its ruin,
Frayed and faded rug (that was *too* red)
Redundant books —
Once their students wore them
For hats, umbrellas, and are now fit
To run their minds naked.

A gauche plant, banished for eccentricities
Of growth — unacceptable
Between smart curtains —
Sprawls relaxed. Nothing more expected,
It may branch birds, clouds.
There is sufficient silence.

Unassailed here. Yet a woman called
Who had lived in this house.
Describing her family's childhood,
Where the sideboard stood, where the piano —
She said, "Two brothers died
In the room where you sort jumble."

Must I elude their deaths — sad boys
Whom I never knew?
Pricing stopped clocks, tired woollies,
I hear their hearts....
The springs rise up; the newt comes alive,

Pricked by the inescapable world.
Those boys may play with any
Books, clocks, umbrellas, that they choose....

WALKING HOME

A room in a bishop's palace.
Diocesan matters
Discreetly filed. Stencils.

In winter, sometimes,
Sunset pouring through an oak — so old,
Arms are chained to head. It flares indignant,
Glinting its bonds. The typewriter answers,
Simmering red.

Why not such fancies? Machine and I
Have done the work, meticulous —
No less efficient
Because sunsets change us.

It is that lonely tasks
Breed fantasies. Years of walking home
Through the great garden, have enriched,
Saved — perhaps from losing "strangeness",
Delicate lens
Tinting the common sight, quickly mislaid
Among computers, systems,
But in a musty room
Facing a freedom of birds and squirrels,
Become an intuition; grace to see
Natural lambency about the creatures.

Some say that people emanate
This shining also. I never saw it outline
Any that I know....

Therefore, it follows — walking home,
I am not luminous to birds and animals
As they to me. My passing means no more

Than the shadow of firs
Brushing out a cold evening coming.
Fir shadow too, in the brown room,
Very sweet all day. One must ignore it
For the work's sake. But afterwards, what harm
If the shadow perceive a sudden flush
Between unhuman things —

The oak, the typewriter
In its business mask —
Were not its steely vitals drawn
Native as oak, from the hot earth?

A thousand blackbirds roost
In the drive bushes. Garden and churchyard
Are one great round — steeped in ceremonial
Long before Christ. Often I feel the rites
Quilling, like blackbirds....

This is an old, holy place,
Waging perpetual wars. I side with them —
But am unsure under what rising powers
I walk home.

SOLVA HARBOUR

Always one hill brilliant and one dark,
In memory — sharing the long curve
To sunset. Seas leap and fall
With a white sigh around two rocks,
Markers and exclaimers
Under whatever sky,
As we are ourselves

When we return, to breathe upon
Fading light. Is such remembering
A life form? Will it revive
Peripheral presences?
Floaters in the iris,
Vague to a central vision
Dazzled with happiness....

Forms we would now acknowledge, name
As witnesses: whether or not aware
On that day, how we sat stunned
In our own silence, like the boats
In the emptied harbour,
Waiting for inflowing tide
To move them again.

There was a girl running to swim
In the evening: she would be old now.
We scarcely noticed her pass
But the years insist, she was beautiful.
We would recreate her
Out of the mindless joy
Through which we sensed her....

She: and the flowers in our colours,
The seabirds. All we did not heed —

Being on that day our own
Adamant life. In a sunned mirror,
Brighter than experienced....
Though it blows up for storm
And the harbour's grey.

AFTERWARDS

Winter. Out of long hiding,
In a filthy coat, by devious ways
He achieved home.
Stared from the courtyard
Down the familiar drive
Into the city. Empty.
The loved horses — that should have pranced him,
In a fine rig, up between arched,
Everlasting trees —
Gone. For he looked.

Door to the kitchens, hanging.
Along bare tables, winter. Winter blown over floors —
A dozen or more crouched here and there,
Old pensioners, in attitudes of waiting.
For what — or whom? For him?

One, near the door, shivered,
Drawing her rags. Spoke up.
"Good day — *citizen!*"

Of all remaining, human and animal,
He the only creature that was young?
His pretty wife — stirring a pot! She, too, grown old?
Word had been brought him that his infant heir
Had died. They did not speak of it.
She cried, "How thin — how thin!"
He answered, "You are beautiful as ever...".

They smiled: like the sun in winter.

Then she, "Rest, now. Take some of this soup —
But it has to go round, these have no one but us
To care for them." And again that woman.
"Share and share alike — *citizen!*"

When spring altered the kitchen shadows,
A crippled garden-man tried to turn earth
For a cabbage plot — no other place than this
Ever in his pattern.

The "citizen", daring sunlight,
Received the beseeching spade into his hand
Like a petition
To the feudal lord. From upsidedown,
Nothing had changed.

The woman by the door — mortally ill —
Accosted him often, in her new pride.
"I shall be gone from here, when my lump heals —
My son will come for me!" A shift of arrogance.
"He went to fight at the barricades...".
Eye to eye, he saw by the fierce blink,
Her pain and his were not unlike.

Long evenings: when all the dependent skeletons,
Resigned to hunger, condemned to equality,
Drowsed. His wife slept too,
Nursing responsibility in her tired arms
As one hugs a child.

Alone with echoes, he would try to mend
His coat-of-arms on the great chimney piece —
Vandalised phoenix and supporting shields —

Then fall idle: knowing he needed the sleepers
As they needed him. Change was merely a flag of truce
At the barricades.

QUESTIONS OF COLOUR

Child in a new house,
Trying the colours.

To stand here: and stand there,
Looking....

Red, blue and yellow rooms.
And one, white.
"She knows *all* her colours...".

And stands, relating to brief experience
The red, the blue

But cannot stay with red,
It brazes innocence
And she runs, afraid.

Yellow floods with sun
As she stares. She has just seen
Somebody angry in the white room —
On the blue wall
A shadow passes,
Hanging down its head.

Now the child's life is coloured.
Years to come
(After she will have finished with this house,
Done with it, moved on)
Colour and blanch, striking uneasy
Wherever she'll meet it,
The blow of white.
Milk, weddings, snow
Will raise allergies: nor will her nature
Trust the heat of the heart's red room

And blue — colour of sky?
But shadows cross it,
Bowed down...?

Yellow, with the sun coming —
Ah, safe in that room!
Shadowless gold to back her joys always,
Vibrate pilgrimage....

Some no-face gives her
A first colour-box. She dips the brush
That never dipped before —
Lets out her breath....

Stripes her identity across and down
Unquestioned paper.

STILLS

I

Images. Plants.
Sleeping figures. Animals in fields.
Eggs, perfect on small shadow.
All deaths....
These wait: mounting like pregnancy
Or war. What is it they expect?

Activating eye. Seed explosion.
Daybreak. Slaughter.
Beak drumming out a star.
Resurrection?

Such fulfilments *will be* —
But the waiting
Transcends.

II

Now, behind cut-outs, this world quickens,
Streaming up satellites, burnishing
Mute expressions of our common lot
Against synthetic radiance.

Progressions — are nothing. Still simplicities
Evoke more.

III

Round the quiescent shapes
As they gather power,
A whip of silence
Guards them from the world.

As when the pure sky
Meets the wild sea,
Ruling a line of sight.
"Thus far...".

Upon the shore, behind the bound sand,
An Eye questions: and concedes.
"No farther...".

ON A PERFORMANCE OF NOYE'S FLUDDE

And when music told us
The Ark was ready,
The town's children came
In heads of lions,
Bears, owls — each animal and bird.

Two by two. Hand in hand.

Their feet on the aisle floor,
Trotting in rhythm,
Thudded like heartbeats.

Why were we so moved?
Was it to do with God
High on a wall, steering the goings-on
In a big, necessary voice?
The children/animals taking so long
To reach, without loss of heads,
The belly of the Ark....

We ourselves had contrived
The wild masks. Paper and paste.
When they began to run, they came alive.

Some of us wept.

Perhaps the very simpleness —
Clunking a row of mugs to express
Imminent storm. "Kyrie eleison"
As a tribal dance. *Was* it so, once
When we were children indeed,
Under God's horns?

Close round the crowded Ark
As we could get, roaring the "Praise God"
Not as a hymn,
More as a splendid yelp
After dangerous work.
The children/animals
Herded to sanctuary. The tempest quelled.

Dark, outside.

Farther down the carpark,
The nuclear bunker. A few still staging
Comfortless protest,
Most of us sick and tired
Of the politics. Back at the church,
Helpers already dismantling
The cardboard Ark.

VISIONARY AIDS

Never seen
Because never thought?

A way. Some thread not pulled through the maze
Though it shine level with the eye.

Sight reinforced by thought
Can work miracles.
Go on — glare, furious enough, at smoke
Lazy from the power station!
Billow it, speed it —
Rolling bouquets of carnation,
Another sunset, if you like,
For the sullen street....

Fierceness of thought was all it took
To do that.

But eye neglects, without slow camera,
How when a drop falls back
Into milk (into grief's wine)
Impact forms a beautiful small crown.

Other exquisites too, things unfolding
Precise being — not at all what they seem
To the unaided glance: a world behind the world —
Once found,
Everything there jewels the looking.

In slowest-motion thought, a seeing comes
That finds us out....

As when it seemed sure, by illumination,
Trees at the full are aware of God.

All day, their tranquil intake focussed,
Centring absolute leaves: the tripod extended,
Exalted, from off the earth.

But night...?
No human eye can read the dark

Unless it use the eye's own afterlight,
Magnified by faith.

THE FOX

Lightfoot on loneliness,
A winter fox

Not hunted
But as the true light in fur is,
Each hair a spirit
Of the whole radiance.
Light and the woods
And revelation
Come all together, as though prophesied.

Later, in weariness,
I dreamed a fox
Running on sparkle. Delicate tread
Indented trackings of mastodon,
Dinosaur — back and back
To infinity's edge. And there the fox sprang off
Into the dark. I saw his diamond brush
Illuminate nothingness.
These imprints faded,
Fused into man's with links of holy fire.

This was the long-expected comet,
Emanuel. God-with-us.

I had not thought
To see that in my time — and was asleep
Only a minute.

RUSHES OF LIFE TO THE HEAD

Sometimes he comes through the house, calling me
And seems obsessed with finding me.

I answer — like a flute? But my voice is old.
Suddenly it is night.

I live such moments as though I had long red hair,
Eyes of hyacinth —
As though the trees of the world
Shook out new leaves, the day before felling.

Do not laugh at us —

We give each other this
Not as we are but as we were once.

Who now remembers us?

In that long room, the vases are full of silence.

ACKNOWLEDGEMENTS

Some of these poems have previously appeared in *Poetry Wales*, *Poetry Review*, *Anglo-Welsh Review*, *PN Review*, and have been broadcast on *Poetry Now*.